MW01641456

MARYLAND BIRD GUIDE

BIRDS OF PREY

Birds of prey are birds that hunt for meat. They have strong hooked beaks, powerful talons and good eyesight.

Osprey

Habitat: Near shallow bodies of water

Diet: Fish, insects, and small mammals

Wingspan: 5 feet

FUN FACT: They have a reversible toe that can grasp with two toes behind and two toes in front.

American Kestrel

Habitat: Deserts, fields, tropical lowlands, and urban areas

Diet: Insects, small rodents, small birds, reptiles, and amphibians

Wingspan: 22 inches

FUN FACT: They are the smallest falcon in North America

Great Horned Owl

Habitat: forests, wetlands, cities, etc.

Diet: Small mammals, other birds, snakes, insects, and frogs

Wingspan: 4.6 feet

FUN FACT: Due to the shape of their wings, they can fly silently and sneak up on their prey.

Barred Owl

Habitat: Dense forests

Diet: Small mammals, other birds, frogs, turtles, chickens, and ducks

Wingspan: 3-4 feet

FUN FACT: Their call sounds like someone calling "who cooks for you, who cooks for you all?

Eastern Screech Owl

Habitat: Forests

Diet: Insects, small rodents, smaller birds, and frogs

Wingspan: 19-24 inches

FUN FACT: They don't actually screech.

Red Shouldered Hawk

Habitat: Forests, wooded streams, and swamps

Diet: Small mammals, other birds, reptiles, and amphibians

Wingspan: 37 – 42 inches

FUN FACT: Their eyesight is eight times more powerful than human's eyesight.

Cooper's Hawk

Habitat:
Forests, fields, and streams

Diet: medium sized birds, small mammals, reptiles, and insects

Wingspan: 29-37 inches

FUN FACT: Females are one third larger than males.

Peregrine Falcon

Habitat: Mountains, forests, cities, valleys, desert, and coastlines

Diet: Other birds, small insects, and small mammals

Wingspan: 2.4 – 3.9 feet

FUN FACT: A peregrine falcon can see at least one mile.

Red Tailed Hawk

Habitat: Fields, mountains, forests, and grasslands

Diet: Small mammals, other birds, snakes, bats, frogs, and insects

Wingspan: 3.4 – 4.8 feet

FUN FACT: A red tailed hawk can fly 120 miles per hour. That's a lot faster than a car!

Bald Eagle

Habitat: Tall trees near bodies of water

Diet: Fish, other birds, and small mammals

Wingspan: 5.9 – 7.5 feet

FUN FACT: The largest nest was 9.5 feet in diameter, 20 feet deep and weighed almost 3 tons.

Barn Owl

Habitat: Grasslands, hay meadows, barns, and farms

Diet: Rodents, small birds, lizards, insects, and frogs

Wingspan: 4 feet

FUN FACT: Barn owls have uneven ears. The left ear is higher than the right.

22

Water birds often have adaptations that allow them to dive and swim to search for food.

Great Blue Heron

Habitat: tall trees to nest in near fresh or brackish water

Diet: Fish, shellfish, frogs, small birds and rodents, and insects

Wingspan: 7 feet

FUN FACT: They are 4 feet tall and only weigh 5 pounds.

Green Heron

Habitat: Lakes, ponds, marshes, swamps, and streamsides

Diet: fish

Wingspan: 26 inches

FUN FACT: The green heron is one of the few birds to use tools.

Great Egret

Habitat: Wetlands, streams, ponds, and marshes

Diet: Fish, crustaceans, frogs, snakes, salamanders, and aquatic insects

Wingspan: 4.3 – 5.6 feet

FUN FACT: They can fly up to 25 miles per hour.

Common Loon

Habitat: Large ponds and wooded lakes

Diet: Fish, aquatic insects, leeches, and frogs

Wingspan: 46 inches

FUN FACT: Loons have solid bones unlike other birds so they can dive easier.

Mallard Duck

Habitat: Water areas

Diet: Insects, shrimp, plants, and seeds

Wingspan: 3 feet

FUN FACT: Feed them oats, birdseed, chopped lettuce, sliced grapes, and frozen peas rather than bread that can harm them.

Laughing Gull

Habitat: Marshes, bays, piers, beaches, and oceans

Diet: Small fish, crustaceans, insects, and horseshoe crab eggs

Wingspan: 37-47 inches

FUN FACT: They are named after their call, which sounds like "Ha ha ha ha".

Canada Goose

Habitat: Lakes, ponds, bays, marshes, and fields

Diet: Grass, seeds, and berries

Wingspan: 4.2 – 6.1 feet

FUN FACT: They are one of the most intelligent birds.

BACKYARD BIRDS

Backyard birds are the ones that are seen on birdfeeders and live in the trees in your backyard

Cardinal

Habitat: Forests, gardens, towns, parks, and grassy fields

Diet: Insects, grasses, berries, and wild fruit

Wingspan: 10 – 12 inches

FUN FACT: One cardinal may have more than a dozen song variations.

American Crow

Habitat: Fields, woodlands, forests, parking lots, city garbage dumps, and towns

Diet: anything it can find, like insects, spiders, snails, earthworms, frogs, small snakes, shellfish, etc.

Wingspan: 2.8 – 3.3 feet

FUN FACT: They are good problem solvers and research shows they remember human faces.

American Robin

Habitat: woodlands, suburban backyards and grasslands

Diet: insects, berries and fruit

Wingspan: 12 – 16 inches

FUN FACT: They have about 2,900 feathers.

Indigo Bunting

Habitat: Woods, roads, powerlines, and bushy and weedy farmlands

Diet: Insects and berries

Wingspan: 7-9 inches

FUN FACT: They migrate at night using the stars to guide them.

Dark Eyed Junco

Habitat: Forests, fields, parks, and backyards

Diet: Seeds and insects

Wingspan 7 – 10 inches

FUN FACT: Their nickname is snowbird because the snowy weather follows them as they migrate.

Song Sparrow

Habitat: Bushy fields, shrubby marshes, woodlands, and gardens

Diet: Insects and seeds

Wingspan: 7.1-10 inches

FUN FACT: There is 1.6 billion sparrows in the world

House Finch

Habitat: forests, grassland and near streams

Diet: seeds, berries and insects

Wingspan: 8 – 10 inches

FUN FACT: They can hang upside while they eat.

Downy Woodpecker

Habitat: suburban yards, forests, and orchards

Diet: insects, beetle larvae, and seeds

Wingspan: 10 – 12 inches

FUN FACT: Woodpeckers can peck into a tree 20 times a second.

House Sparrow

Habitat: Forests, meadows, grasslands, deserts, woodlands, cities, parks, and backyards

Diet: Grains, seeds, our dropped food, and insects

Wingspan: 9 inches

FUN FACT: They live on every continent except Antarctica.

Kingbird

Habitat: open spaces in trees

Diet: insects and fruit

Wingspan: 15.5 inches

FUN FACT: A kingbird got its name because it is like a tyrant or king and will defend its nest against larger birds.

Red Winged Black Bird

Habitat: Marshes, wooded swamps, hayfields, and muddy areas

Diet: Beetles, caterpillars, grasshoppers, spiders, millipedes, snails, seeds, and berries

Wingspan: 12 – 16 inches

FUN FACT: One male may have up to 15 different nests.

Mockingbird

Habitat: forest edges, parks and open areas

Diet: berries, fruits and insects.

Wingspan: 12 – 14 inches

FUN FACT: It can sing over 200 songs. It can copy other birds, insects and even electronic songs.

European Starling

Habitat: Cities and suburban areas

Diet: Insects, berries, fruits, and seeds

Wingspan: 12 – 17 inches

FUN FACT: In the 1890s, people decided to bring all the European birds that Shakespeare mentions in his plays and poems. They released them in Central Park, NYC. The European Starlings spread quickly.

Red Bellied Woodpecker

Habitat: woodlands and forests

Diet: Tree frogs, eggs of small birds, oozing sap and even small fish

Wingspan: 15 – 18 inches

FUN FACT: It can stick its tongue out two inches.

Carolina Chickadee

Habitat: forests, swamps, and leafy trees.

Diet: seeds, berries and small fruits

Wingspan: 6 – 8 inches

FUN FACT: They like coconut!

Blue Jay

Habitat: dense forests, especially oak trees

Diet: acorns, beech nuts, seeds, grains, berries and small fruits

Wingspan: 13 -17 inches

FUN FACT: They typically fly around 20 to 25 miles per hour.

Ruby throated Hummingbird

Habitat: tropical rainforests, meadows, forests, mountain tops, and deserts.

Diet: small insects, sugar water, flowers, and spiders.

Wingspan: 4.25 inches

FUN FACT: They wings beat 10 to 15 times per second.

Tufted Titmouse

Habitat: forests, orchards, parks and suburban

Diet: insects, seeds, spiders, snails, eggs and pupae.

Wingspan: 8 – 10 inches

FUN FACT:

The tufted titmouse store seeds in tree cracks or under items on the ground

Eastern Bluebird

Habitat: forest and ponds

Diet: insects, berries, earthworms, snails, tree frogs and small lizards

Wingspan: 10 – 13 inches

FUN FACT: They can spot caterpillars in tall grass from 50 yards away.

Northern Flicker

Habitat: Woodlands, city parks, and suburbs

Diet: Insects, fruits, and seeds

Wingspan: 18-21 inches

FUN FACT: Unlike other woodpeckers, they eat their food from the ground. They use their long barbed tongue to catch ants.

Barn Swallow

Habitat: Meadows, fields, and farmyards

Diet: Insects

Wingspan: 12.5-13.5 inches

FUN FACT: In some cultures if a barn swallow builds a nest in a barn it is considered good luck.

Yellow Throated Warbler

Habitat: forests, swamps, and woodlands near streams

Diet: insects and spiders

Wingspan: 8.3 inches

FUN FACT: Their nest is cup shaped.

Common Grackle

Habitat: Open woodlands

Diet: Insects, small rodents, eggs of other birds, and frogs

Wingspan: 14-18 inches

FUN FACT: They have been seen stealing a worm from a robin's beak.

Common Yellow Throat

Habitat: Swamps, marshes, and overgrown fields

Diet: Insects and seeds

Wingspan: 5.9-7.5 inches

FUN FACT: **They only weight 0.34 ounces.**

Mourning Dove

Habitat: farms, towns, grasslands, and woods

Diet: seeds, grains, grass, insects and snails

Wingspan: 15 to 18 inches

FUN FACT: It is called a mourning dove because its call sounds very sad.

Pileated Woodpecker

Habitat: Forests, wooded parks, and large trees

Diet: Insects, fruits, nuts, larvae, and berries

Wingspan: 30 inches

FUN FACT: Their bill is like a chisel and leaves behind rectangle shaped marks in trees.

Carolina Wren

Habitat: Woodlands

Diet: Insects

Wingspan: 11 inches

FUN FACT: The male and females sing different parts of a song at the same time so it will sound like only one bird singing.

White Breasted Nuthatch

Habitat: Forests, groves, and shade trees

Diet: Insects and seeds

Wingspan: 7.9 – 10.6 inches

FUN FACT: They have a backward-facing toe that helps them go upside down on a tree.

White Throated Sparrow

Habitat: Forests

Diet: Seeds and insects

Wingspan: 9.1 inches

FUN FACT: They are one of the few birds that sing at night.

Goldfinch

Habitat: weedy fields, orchards, forests, plains and backyards

Diet: seeds, insects, maple sap, and buds.

Wingspan: 7.5 – 8.7 inches

FUN FACT: When they are about to fly, their songs sounds like "po-ta-to-chip.

Gray Catbird

Habitat: Swamps, bushy fields, bushes in gardens, and leafy areas along woods and streams

Diet: Insects and berries

Wingspan: 11 inches

FUN FACT: They can sing up to 100 songs

Chipping Sparrow

Habitat: Open woodlands

Diet: Seeds and insects

Wingspan: 8-9 inches

FUN FACT: Sparrows can swim when threatened.

Brown Headed Cowbird

Habitat: Grasslands

Diet: Seeds and insects

Wingspan: 12-15 inches

FUN FACT: Cowbirds lay their eggs in other birds' nests. The other birds raise their babies.

HOW TO HELP THE BIRDS

Birds need your help to stay healthy and safe!

Only feed them the correct food. A change in their diet can be harmful.

Bread is especially bad for birds!

If you find a nestling,
if you can, return it to its nest.

If you find a fledging, leave them where you find them unless they're in a dangerous spot.

If you find an injured bird, please contact local rescues or wildlife rehabilitator for their advice. Do not give them water or food.

Make sure to remove trash you see outside – especially fishing line!

INDEX

Index of Birds

Index of Birds

Made in the USA
Monee, IL
03 February 2023

e5bb3e46-76a4-4f92-9366-d0325b1366c6R01